What are birds of prey?

Birds that hunt and eat other animals are called birds of prey. They get their name because 'prey' means animals that are hunted. Another name for them is 'raptor', meaning 'thief'. Birds of prey have powerful claws for grabbing prey and sharp beaks for tearing up meat.

Discover

Look in books or on the Internet to discover what other animals were also known as 'raptors'.

Jackal buzzard

Are there lots of different kinds?

There are about 300 types of birds of prey. They include mighty eagles and soaring vultures, tiny falconets, and falcons such as the peregrine. Hawks, buzzards and kites are birds of prey, and so are owls, which hunt at night.

Long-billed vulture

Philippine eagle

Saker falcon

Broken bones

Birds of prey fly boldly through trees and around cliffs to chase their prey. They can end up crashing, and perhaps breaking some bones.

Why do vultures fly in circles?

Because they are always looking for food! Unlike other birds of prey, vultures do not kill their own food. Instead, they feed on the bodies of dead animals. They will also circle sick or injured animals, waiting for them to die.

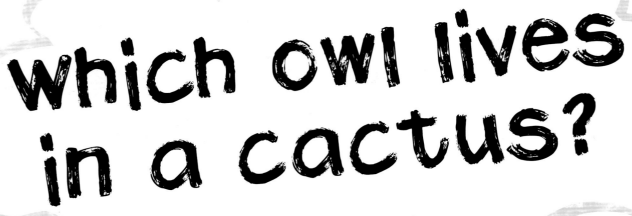

Which owl lives in a cactus?

Elf owl

The elf owl does. This tiny owl lives in Mexico and the United States. It makes its nest inside a hole in a spiny plant called a cactus, or sometimes a tree. The owl doesn't make the hole itself, but usually finds an old empty one made by a woodpecker.

Why do eagles like the seaside?

Some types of eagle live near the sea because it's a great place to find food. These include bald eagles, as well as white-tailed eagles and Steller's sea eagles. They hunt for fish in the water but also swoop on seabirds, squid and even seals.

Bald eagles

In the freezer

Gyrfalcons live in the icy Arctic, and often keep a store of frozen food for their chicks. They break bits off with their beaks when they are hungry.

Do barn owls live in barns?

Yes they do! Barn owls often make their homes in buildings such as barns, church steeples and old ruins. Barns are especially good homes because they are used to store grain, so often attract mice and rats – an owl's favourite food!

Listen

On dark nights, especially in the countryside, listen out for an owl's hooting call.

Why do kestrels hover?

Kestrel

Hovering helps a kestrel to spot food. It hovers in one spot in mid-air like a helicopter. This helps the kestrel's head stay still, so the bird can spot prey such as mice and lizards. A kestrel hovers by flying into a gentle wind.

How strong are birds of prey?

Golden eagles and Eurasian eagle owls are incredibly strong. They can grab animals such as hares, foxes, sheep and goats, or even young deer. If the prey isn't too heavy, they will try to carry it away.

Eagle

Look out!

Bald eagles and crowned eagles sometimes attack humans, especially when guarding young chicks. But they don't kill or eat them.

Can eagles fly without flapping?

Eagles and some other birds of prey can fly long distances with their wings stretched out, like a plane. Instead of flapping, they find patches of warm air, called thermals. The warm air rises upwards, carrying the birds as they glide along.

Pretend
Spread your arms out wide and pretend you are an eagle soaring through the sky.

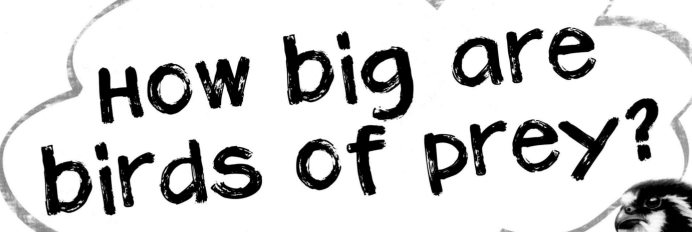

How big are birds of prey?

Birds of prey can be bigger than other birds – but they vary a lot. The biggest is the Andean condor, a type of vulture with a wingspan up to 3 metres across. One of the smallest is the black-thighed falconet, which is just 15 centimetres long.

Black-thighed falconet

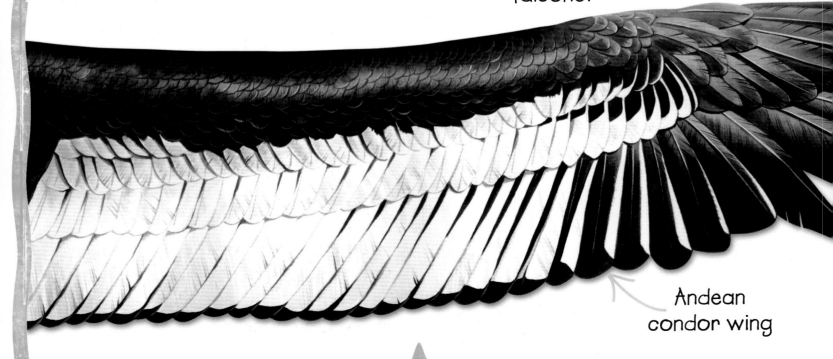

Andean condor wing

Why do eagles fight snakes?

So they can eat them up! The short-toed snake eagle battles with snakes up to 1.5 metres long, biting and clawing at them as they wriggle. The eagle usually wins, and eats the snake head-first.

Short-toed snake eagle

Measure

Stretch out your arms sideways and ask someone to measure your 'wingspan' with a tape measure.

Time to fly!

Lesser spotted eagles fly all the way from Europe to southern Africa every year. They can cover almost 300 kilometres every day.

Which bird of prey eats ducks for dinner?

White-tailed eagles do! Ducks are among their favourite prey. They are quite easy for the eagle to catch as it swoops over the surface of a lake or a river. These eagles also live along coasts where they hunt for seabirds.

Why do kestrels perch near roads?

To look for something tasty to eat! Motorway verges are left to grow wild. They are home to the kestrel's prey of birds, lizards and insects, so kestrels are often seen near busy roads. These birds of prey have also learnt to hunt in city parks, and even build their nests in towns.

Kestrel

HOW high can a vulture fly?

Vultures are the highest-flying birds of prey. An Andean condor can soar at up to 5000 metres above sea level, over the Andes Mountains. One Ruppell's griffon vulture was found flying at 11,000 metres – higher than Mount Everest!

Andean condor

Horrible harpies

Harpy eagles may get their name from the harpies, winged monsters from Greek mythology. They looked like evil birds with women's faces, and they snatched people's food.

Can owls use feathers to hear?

Yes, as well as ears, owls use feathers to hear. They have special feathers on their faces that help to reflect the sound of their prey to their ears. Owls also have fluffy feathers that muffle the sound of their wings.

LOOK
Next time you're in a car on a motorway, look out for kestrels perched nearby.

How do owls go fishing?

Fishing owls swoop over the water and grab fish, or wade in to catch them swimming by. Blakiston's fish owl is one of the biggest owls. It can be 75 centimetres in height and weigh 4.5 kilograms — and it can catch fish almost as big as itself!

Blakiston's fish owl

Measure
With a tape measure, work out how big a nest 4 metres high and 2.5 metres wide would look.

Which eagle builds a giant nest?

The bald eagle does. Eagles build their nests on cliffs or in treetops. Every year, they return to the same nest and add more branches on top. Over time, the nest grows huge! Some bald eagle nests are 4 metres high and 2.5 metres across.

Bald eagle nest

Fish feast

Some birds of prey can catch up to 20 fish every day, especially when they have chicks to feed.

Why do falcons stoop?

When falcons suddenly zoom down from the sky it is called 'stooping'. They do this to take their prey by surprise. The peregrine falcon has the fastest stoop speed of all – it can plunge towards the ground at 350 kilometres an hour – faster than a speeding train.

How fast do baby birds grow up?

Birds of prey chicks grow up very quickly. At five weeks old, chicks learn to fly and can leave the nest. By the age of two, they are adults and can have their own chicks.

1. Chick hatches

2. Two days old

3. Four weeks old

4. Six months old

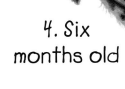

Peregrine falcon

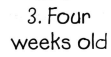

Swallow-tailed kite

When is a bird like a kite?

When it's a bird of prey! Kites are fast, sleek birds that have pointed wings and forked tails. They feed on mice, rats, lizards or fish. These birds get their name because of the way they hover and flutter in the air.

Hiding out

Some people hunt birds of prey or steal their eggs. To stop this, many species are protected by law and their nesting sites are kept secret.

Draw

Look for pictures of Argentavis in books or on the Internet. Draw one of your own.

Argentavis

Which raptor was as big as a plane?

Six million years ago, a giant bird of prey called *Argentavis* ruled the skies. It was similar to a condor, but with a wingspan of 7 metres — bigger than some small planes.

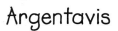

Do birds of prey have eagle eyes?

Birds of prey have brilliant eyesight – they really are 'eagle-eyed'. Even from high in the sky, they can see mice or lizards on the ground, or fish underwater. Some hawks and eagles can see about five times better than a human can.

Peregrine falcon

which bird is king of the vultures?

This big vulture from South America is called the king vulture. Its bright colours make it easy to recognize. Ancient people believed it was one of their gods, which might be how it got its name.

King vulture

How can a kite eat a snail?

The snail kite is a small bird of prey that feeds on water snails. It has a very curved, hooked beak for taking the snails out of their shells.

Ready to serve

The sharp-shinned hawk takes its prey to a special perch to remove the skin and tear up the meat. Then it carries the best bits to its nest to eat.

Ask

People eat snails too. If you haven't tried them, ask friends or family if they have. Did they taste nice?

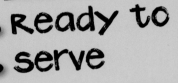

Why do vultures have bald heads?

Having a bald head helps vultures to stay clean. Vultures mainly eat carrion, or dead animals. They bite through the skin, then stick their heads inside the body to nibble at the rotting flesh. Their heads have no feathers to stop rotting meat sticking to them.

Vulture

stinky supper

Most raptors have a poor sense of smell, but turkey vultures are super-sniffers. They can track down dead animals to eat by following their smell.

can an eagle kill a man?

No, eagles can't kill people. But according to legend, an ancient Greek poet died when an eagle mistook his bald head for a stone, and dropped a tortoise on it. Some birds of prey do this to try to break tortoises open.

HOW do owls see in the dark?

Owls have big eyes that are very good at sensing light. Human eyes can detect white light and colour. But owls mainly see just the difference between dark and light. Their night vision is up to 100 times better than ours.

Great horned owl

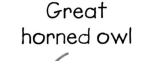

LOOK

Try looking at this book in almost darkness. Can you still see the colours properly?

Why do secretaries stamp?

Secretary birds are unusual-looking birds of prey with long, thin legs. They kill snakes and other prey by pecking and stamping on them. Their name comes from the feathers on their heads, which look like the quill pens that secretaries used long ago.

Make

Ask an adult to cut a straw diagonally to make a pointed 'quill' pen. Dip it in paint to write with.

Secretary bird

Do vultures throw stones?

Some vultures do! Egyptian vultures are one of the few animals to use tools. They sometimes eat other birds' eggs, but can't crack them open with their beaks. Instead they pick up stones and throw them at the eggs to break them.

Egyptian vulture

Royal birds

Gyrfalcons are found in the Arctic. Royalty in Egypt and China used to keep them as pets. It was said only a king could hunt with a gyrfalcon.

When do chicks fight each other?

Golden eagles usually lay two eggs at a time. When the chicks hatch, they often start to fight each other for food and space in the nest. Sometimes, the bigger chick kicks the smaller one out!

How do owls see upside down?

By twisting their long, bendy necks owls can see upside down! Their eyeballs are not round, and cannot swivel in their sockets. So to look in different directions, owls have to turn their heads right around, and almost upside down.

Baby owl

Peregrine falcon

when do falcons wear hoods?

Falcons might wear a hood when they hunt for people. This is called falconry. Falconers sometimes use hoods to cover their falcon's heads as this helps to keep them calm. The hoods are often beautifully made and decorated.

Mini owl

The elf owl is the smallest owl, and one of the smallest birds of prey. It's just 14 centimetres long and could sit in your hand.

why do people watch birds?

Birdwatchers are people who love the beauty of birds, and like to spot different bird species. Some keep lists and tick off all the birds they have seen. The rarer a bird is, the more they want to see it!

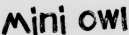

watch

Try birdwatching in your garden or nearest park. Note down what each bird you see looks and sounds like.

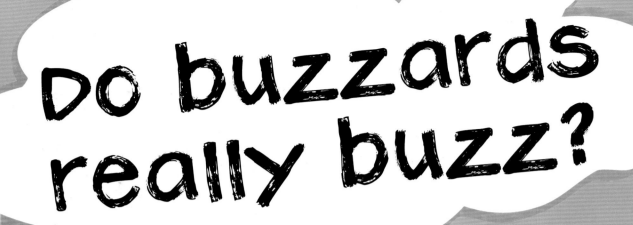

Do buzzards really buzz?

Various birds of prey have the name 'buzzard', including the common buzzard, the lizard buzzard and the honey buzzard. But buzzards don't buzz! They are said to get their name from an old word meaning 'stupid', because they cannot be trained by falconers.

Honey buzzard

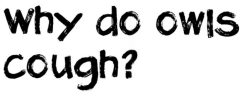

Why do owls cough?

Owls cough to get rid of waste from their food. They swallow small animals whole, but cannot digest parts such as bones and fur. These collect into a lump inside the owl, called a pellet. The owl coughs the pellet up to get rid of it.

Owl coughing up pellet

Aerial acrobats

Some raptors are amazing acrobats. They can swoop, dive, spiral and somersault in the air to chase prey, or to show off their skills to a mate.

Can hawks help people?

Birds of prey can be very useful for farmers who want to scare smaller birds away from their crops. They are also used to scare flocks of birds away from airports, where they can damage aircraft that are taking off.

Visit

Falconers sometimes take trained birds to fairs, shows or fetes. See if you can visit one of these events.

can owls go to the movies?

They did in 2010! *Legend of the Guardians: The Owls of Ga'Hoole* is an animated film. It tells the story of a young owl and how he tries to save owl-kind from its enemies. Film-makers copied how real owls behave to make the animated ones look as real.

Do birds of prey hunt with weapons?

Yes, a raptor's weapons are part of its body — its razor-sharp talons and strong beak. Both are made of keratin, the same hard substance as our fingernails. But they are much tougher and sharper, and are used to tear and slash at prey.

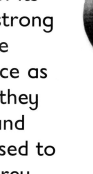

Beak

 Talons

Think
Your fingernails are the human version of talons. We don't use them as weapons, but what are they useful for?

on the money
The bald eagle is the national bird of the USA and appears on some of its coins, such as this dollar coin.

Why do secretary birds hunt in pairs?

Secretary birds often hunt in pairs or sometimes small groups. This makes finding and catching food easier. They spread out, looking for small prey animals. Once one bird finds something, the others help to catch and kill it.

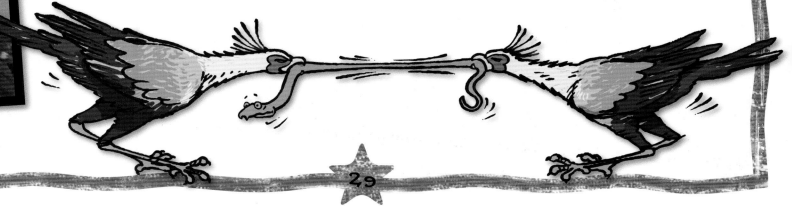

Quiz time

Do you remember what you have read about birds of prey? Here are some questions to test your memory. The pictures will help you. If you get stuck, read the pages again.

page 12

3. Why do kestrels perch near roads?

4. Why do falcons stoop?

page 15

1. Why do vultures fly in circles?

page 5

5. How fast do baby birds grow up?

page 16

2. Can eagles fly without flapping?

page 9

6. When is a bird like a kite?

page 17

page 17

11. When do falcons wear hoods?

page 25

7. Which raptor was as big as a plane?

page 19

12. Can hawks help people?

page 27

8. Which bird is king of the vultures?

13. Do birds of prey hunt with weapons?

page 29

9. Why do secretaries stamp?

page 22

10. When do chicks fight each other?

page 23

Answers

1. To look for dead animals on the ground
2. Yes, they can glide along on warm air
3. To look for small animals to eat in roadside verges
4. To take their prey by surprise
5. They grow up very quickly
6. A kite is a bird of prey that hovers and flutters in the sky
7. Argentavis
8. The king vulture
9. To kill prey such as snakes
10. Eagle chicks fight for space in the nest
11. When they need to stay calm
12. Yes, they can help farmers
13. Yes, they have talons and claws

Index